Wrong Way!

by Claire Daniel
illustrated by Bill Petersen

Harcourt
SCHOOL PUBLISHERS

Printed in China

ISBN 10: 0-15-350538-9
ISBN 13: 978-0-15-350538-6

Ordering Options
ISBN 10: 0-15-350335-1 (Grade 5 Below-Level Collection)
ISBN 13: 978-0-15-350335-1 (Grade 5 Below-Level Collection)
ISBN 10: 0-15-357534-4 (package of 5)
ISBN 13: 978-0-15-357534-1 (package of 5)

11 12 13 14 15   0940   12 11 10

I admit I was very nervous about my first soccer game playing for the Giants. Even so, I have no idea how something this embarrassing could have happened. There is really no good reason for the humiliation that I experienced that day.

I was new to the school that fall. In fact, it was only the fifth day of school in early September. I had moved from a city school in Atlanta, Georgia. Now my family lived on the fringe of Austin, Texas. Even though we have a lot of family in Austin, we had resided in Atlanta because of Mom and Dad's jobs. Now we're back home with our family.

I don't like it. I know I should be happy, but I miss Atlanta. I like the Atlanta Braves. I like the hamburgers in Atlanta. I like the Atlanta subway, and I even like the Atlanta traffic. I just like Atlanta.

In Atlanta, I was the best player on the soccer team. I'm good, and I am proud to be good. When I tried out for the soccer team here, the coach took one look at me and assigned me to the first team. There was no hesitating on his part.

The first game was really fun. Well, at least it was until the end. I played forward, and I was really doing well. I had high expectations of myself, and I played hard. Everyone else played hard, too, and everyone was enjoying themselves. There were only four minutes left in the game. The other team had possession of the ball, and everyone was in the center of the field.

Suddenly, the ball was loose on the field, and I was nearest to it. My foot kicked it, and I had control. I dribbled the ball down the field a little way. When I saw a large tree like the one on the fringes of the field in Atlanta, in the background, I headed for it, with the ball ahead of me. It was a straight shot to the goal. No one was in between, so I kicked the ball as hard as I could.

My teammates looked stunned. I assumed they had never seen such playing. Boy, was I wrong about that! I slowly figured out what had happened. I had kicked the ball into the opponent's goal.

The next day at school was a nightmare. "Hi, 'Wrong Way'!" a kid yelled before school started. I did not even know the boy. I wanted to crawl in the nearest hole.

Somehow I got through my morning classes. Then it was time for lunch. Oh, my! Lunchtime was sure to be another test. The lunchroom was full of kids, and I still did not know a single soul. I got my tray and sat down by myself. The food did not look too awful. I was actually enjoying my meal, so I did not even notice a girl sitting next to me until she spoke up.

"I saw the game yesterday," she said quietly.

"You and the entire world," I replied.

"It wasn't that bad," she said.

"Yes, I suppose so, if you were a player for the Lions," I joked.

"I watch a lot of soccer games," she said.

"Good for you," I said. I didn't want to give her an opportunity to make fun of me.

"My name is Mary," she said.

I said, "My name is 'Wrong Way,' in case you haven't heard."

"Do your parents call you that?" she asked.

I answered, "No, they call me Mehra."

"Hey," she said, "your name sounds a lot like mine. Mary and Mehra. They are very similar."

"Why do you care whether our names sound alike?" I asked.

"I'm trying to be friendly," she said.

"Sorry," I said. "I guess I'm not feeling too friendly today."

Then she said, "Like I said, I see quite a lot of soccer games, and before my accident, I played on the school team."

I glanced at the far side of her seat. Two crutches leaned against the table. Now I really felt bad about being so rude to her.

"Sorry," I said. "What happened?"

"I fell out of a tree," she said. "It was a silly accident." She picked up her crutches and studied them. Then she said, "I miss soccer. However, I'll heal soon, and I'll be back on the team this spring."

Then Mary said, "I watched you play. You are a very good player. You are quick on your feet, and you keep your eye on the ball. Even if it was the wrong goal, you know how to kick." I looked at her face. She seemed sincere. It made me feel good about myself.

"You shouldn't feel so bad," she coaxed. "You know what they say?"

"What do they say?" I asked.

"If you fall off a horse, you should get right back on."

That afternoon, I forced my legs to walk to the soccer field. As I approached the field, I looked up into the stands, and I saw my dad. Two rows above him, I spotted Mary. After she waved at me, I lifted my arm high and gave her a big wave.

Once we started playing, I had a good time, and no one said a thing about the game yesterday. I didn't score, but I played well.

After the game, I was walking toward the parking lot. Just then, Justin, the captain of the team, stopped me.

He said, "Hey, 'Wrong Way'! You don't mind if we call you that, do you? My name is 'Eyeballs.' I missed the ball a lot last year because I took my eyes off of it."

Another boy joined Justin. He said, "My name is 'Grumpy.' I tend to complain a lot when we have to run laps."

Justin said, "Only the best players get nicknames."

I was stunned. I said, "You think I'm a good player?"

"Oh, yeah," Justin said. "We just need to get you a compass."

"Welcome to the team, 'Wrong Way'!" 'Grumpy' said.

Think Critically

1. What words would you use to describe Mehra?

2. What word on page 3 means almost the same thing as *edge*?

3. When Mehra met Mary, he was not friendly to her. Why do you think he acted that way?

4. Why did Mehra decide to show up for the second game?

5. Has anything ever happened to you that is similar to when Mehra ran the wrong way? Explain your answer.

 Health

Journal Your Goals Name a short-term health goal and a long-term health goal that you have set for yourself. Write a journal entry about how you might achieve these goals.

School-Home Connection Retell the story in *Wrong Way* to a family member or friend. Then ask the person to recall a time when he or she did something embarrassing. Ask what happened as a result.

Word Count: 1,010